Merry Christmas
don't buy this bo

MW00399820

45 cards for expressing all your Christmas wishes if you have any.

STERLING INNOVATION
An imprint of Sterling Publishing Co., Inc.

New York / London
www.sterlingpublishing.com

STERLING, the Sterling logo, STERLING INNOVATION, and the Sterling Innovation logo
are registered trademarks of Sterling Publishing Co., Inc.

10 9 8 7 6 5 4 3 2 1

Published by Sterling Publishing Co., Inc.
387 Park Avenue South, New York, NY 10016
© 2009 someecards, Inc.

Distributed in Canada by Sterling Publishing
C/o Canadian Manda Group, 165 Dufferin Street
Toronto, Ontario, Canada M6K 3H6
Distributed in the United Kingdom by GMC Distribution Services
Castle Place, 166 High Street, Lewes, East Sussex, England BN7 IXU
Distributed in Australia by Capricorn Link (Australia) Pty. Ltd.
P.O. Box 704, Windsor, NSW 2756, Australia

Sterling ISBN 978-1-4027-6809-5

For information about custom editions, special sales, premium and
corporate purchases, please contact Sterling Special Sales
Department at 800-805-5489 or specialsales@sterlingpublishing.com.

Introduction

Ready to jump into the holiday spirit of irksome gift giving, inexplicable melancholy, and rampant alcohol abuse? Then the someecards Christmas book is possibly for you! Finally, you can say goodbye to the hours you're forced to spend looking at generic Christmas cards with glitter-covered angels, glitter-covered elves, and elf-angels with tiny sprinklings of glitter. These tear-out postcards express just the right Christmas sentiment to loved ones, liked ones, mandatory ones, and anyone else who may have issues with elves!

Can't afford stamps because all your money went to gifts and a three-week bender that began a few days before Thanksgiving? Then spread the holiday spirit by putting these cards on your office door, your Christmas tree, or a complete stranger's windshield. Maybe even give one to the bartender who recently requested you stop coming to your favorite pub!

And don't forget that the someecards Christmas book is the perfect stocking stuffer or Secret Santa gift. You'd be hard-pressed to find a simpler and more affordable way to say, "I'm wittier and more resourceful than you." Isn't that what the holidays are all about?

someecards

I'm still confused by the story of Christmas.

_____

_____

_____

_____

som**ee**cards

I hope your Christmas display doesn't incinerate your home and loved ones.

someecards

some**ee**cards

You're a hard person to half-assedly shop for.

_____

_____

_____

_____

some**ee**cards

someecards

Your gift to me was so wonderful
that I think you've
been cheating.

som**ee**cards

someecards

Just wanted to help spread hope, peace, joy, and other marketing buzzwords.

someecards

There's nothing like holiday cheer to offset devastating seasonal affective disorder.

_____

_____

_____

_____

som**ee**cards

Enjoy the holiday
that's technically
not yours.

someecards

_____

_____

_____

_____

som**ee**cards

You'll know I'm your Secret Santa if you don't get anything.

_____

_____

_____

_____

som**ee**cards

I can't wait to have a flamboyantly dressed stranger grope my children.

_____

_____

_____

_____

som<ee>cards

_____

_____

_____

_____

somee cards

I want a menorah for Christmas.

_____

_____

_____

_____

som ee cards

Let's talk about volunteering at a homeless shelter but not actually do it.

someecards

It's the time of the year to start dropping hints at what you want for Christmas.

_____

_____

_____

_____

somee cards

Let's not break up
until after
the holidays.

someecards

I'm going to regift something special for you.

_____

_____

_____

_____

someecards

I really don't feel like carrying all this shit.

_____

_____

_____

_____

som**ee**cards

I am indebted to you and several credit card companies.

_____

_____

_____

_____

som**ee**cards

_____

_____

_____

_____

some**ee**cards

someecards

someecards

Let's not get each other gifts unless you already got me one.

_____

_____

_____

_____

som**ee**cards

I want you to have something
I don't need anymore.

_____

_____

_____

_____

some ee cards

Your gift will
be arriving
late or never.

someecards

I don't particularly care if you've been naughty or nice.

_____

_____

_____

_____

som ee cards

I may not show
up this year.

som**ee**cards

Everyone puts on a few pounds during the holidays.

someecards

I'm too cheap
to buy you
something.

someecards

I'm keeping
the gifts.

someecards

someecards

som**ee**cards

I want a Christmas tree for Hanukkah.

someecards

Best wishes on
your Pan-African
alternative holiday
to Christmas.

someecards

© 2009 someecards, Inc.

Let me know where you think you'll end up New Year's Eve.

som**ee**cards

_____

_____

_____

_____

som**ee**cards

My resolution is to spend more time avoiding friends and family.

someecards

someecards

My resolution is for you to lose weight.

som**ee**cards

Let's put significant pressure on ourselves to have a fun New Year's Eve.

someecards

Let's resolve to repeat last year's mistakes.

someecards